HAL•LEONARD

Piano Play-Along

PIANO | VOCAL | GUITAR • CD   **VOLUME 12**

CHRISTMAS FAVORITES

T0052583

ISBN 978-0-634-08193-4

HAL•LEONARD®
CORPORATION
7777 W. BLUEMOUND RD. P.O. BOX 13819 MILWAUKEE, WI 53213

Visit Hal Leonard Online at
www.halleonard.com

CONTENTS

BLUE CHRISTMAS

Words and Music by BILLY HAYES
and JAY JOHNSON

Moderately

I'll have a blue Christ-mas, with-out you. _____ I'll be so

blue think-ing a-bout you. _____ Dec-o-ra-tions of

red on a green Christ-mas tree won't mean a thing if

THE CHRISTMAS SONG
(Chestnuts Roasting on an Open Fire)

Music and Lyric by MEL TORME
and ROBERT WELLS

10

DO YOU HEAR WHAT I HEAR

Words and Music by NOEL REGNEY
and GLORIA SHAYNE

HERE COMES SANTA CLAUS
(Right Down Santa Claus Lane)

Words and Music by GENE AUTRY
and OAKLEY HALDEMAN

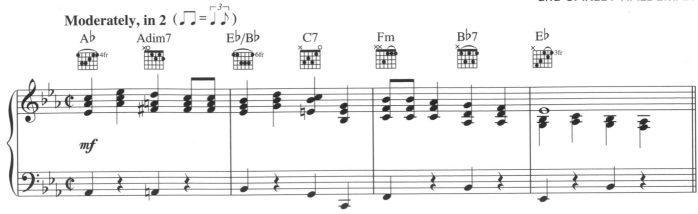

Here comes San-ta Claus! Here comes San-ta Claus! Right down San-ta Claus Lane!

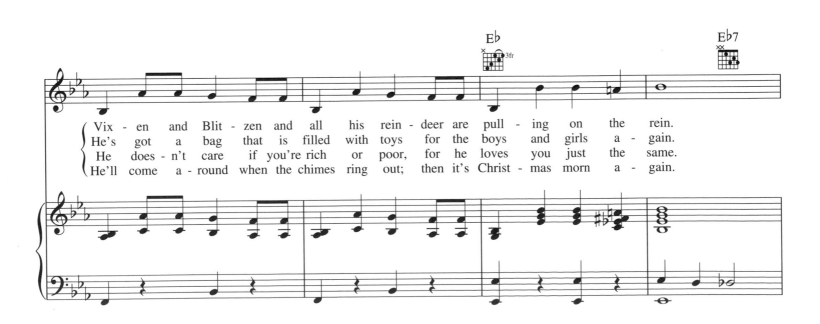

Vix-en and Blit-zen and all his rein-deer are pull-ing on the rein.
He's got a bag that is filled with toys for the boys and girls a-gain.
He does-n't care if you're rich or poor, for he loves you just the same.
He'll come a-round when the chimes ring out; then it's Christ-mas morn a-gain.

Bells are ring - ing, chil - dren sing - ing, all is mer - ry and
Hear those sleigh - bells jin - gle jan - gle, what a beau - ti - ful
San - ta knows that we're God's chil - dren; that makes ev - 'ry - thing
Peace on earth will come to all if we just fol - low the

bright.
sight. Hang your stock - ings and say your pray'rs,
right. Jump in bed, cov - er up your head, } 'cause
light. Fill your hearts with a Christ - mas cheer,
Let's give thanks to the Lord a - bove, }

San - ta Claus comes to - night. San - ta Claus comes to - night.

I SAW MOMMY KISSING SANTA CLAUS

Words and Music by
TOMMIE CONNOR

MERRY CHRISTMAS, DARLING

Words and Music by RICHARD CARPENTER
and FRANK POOLER

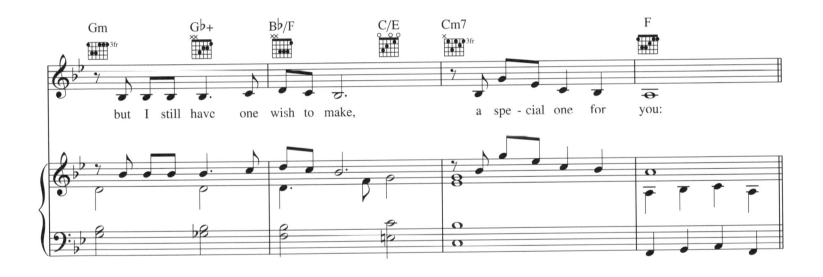

20

LET IT SNOW! LET IT SNOW! LET IT SNOW!

Words by SAMMY CAHN
Music by JULE STYNE

Oh, the weath-er out-side is fright-ful, but the fire is so de-light-ful, and since we've no place to go, let it snow! let it snow! let it snow!

It does-n't show signs of stop-ping, and I fi-re is slow-ly dy-ing and, my

SILVER BELLS
from the Paramount Picture THE LEMON DROP KID

Words and Music by JAY LIVINGSTON
and RAY EVANS

The Ultimate Songbooks!

Christmas Collections

From Hal Leonard

All books arranged for piano, voice, & guitar.

Christmas Time Is Here
A 50-song Christmas collection! Includes: As Long as There's Christmas • Caroling, Caroling • The Christmas Song • Christmas Time Is Here • Do You Hear What I Hear • Emmanuel • Feliz Navidad • Let's Make It Christmas All Year 'Round • The Most Wonderful Time of the Year • Santa Baby • Silver Bells • and more!
00310761 ....$16.95

The Best Christmas Songs Ever - 3rd Edition
A collection of more than 70 of the best-loved songs of the season, including: Blue Christmas • Frosty the Snow Man • Grandma Got Run Over by a Reindeer • I'll Be Home for Christmas • Jingle-Bell Rock • Rudolph, The Red-Nosed Reindeer • Silver Bells • You're All I Want for Christmas • and many more.
00359130 ....$19.95

The Big Book Of Christmas Songs
An outstanding collection of over 120 all-time Christmas favorites and hard-to-find classics. Features: Angels We Have Heard on High • As Each Happy Christmas • Auld Lang Syne • The Boar's Head Carol • Bring a Torch Jeannette, Isabella • Carol of the Bells • Coventry Carol • Deck the Halls • The First Noel • The Friendly Beasts • God Rest Ye Merry Gentlemen • I Heard the Bells on Christmas Day • It Came Upon a Midnight Clear • Jesu, Joy of Man's Desiring • Joy to the World • Masters in This Hall • O Holy Night • The Story of the Shepherd • 'Twas the Night Before Christmas • What Child Is This? • and many more. Includes guitar chord frames.
00311520 ....$19.95

Season's Greetings
A great big collection of 50 favorites, including: All I Want for Christmas Is You • Blue Christmas • The Christmas Song • Frosty the Snow Man • Grandma Got Run Over by a Reindeer • Happy Holiday • I'll Be Home for Christmas • Most of All I Wish You Were Here • Silver Bells • What Made the Baby Cry? • and more.
00310426 ....$16.95

Christmas Songs For Kids
27 songs kids love to play during the holidays, including: Away in a Manger • The Chipmunk Song • Deck the Hall • The First Noel • Jingle Bells • Joy to the World • O Christmas Tree • Silent Night • and more.
00311571 ....$7.95

Contemporary Christian Christmas
20 songs as recorded by today's top Christian artists, including: Michael W. Smith (All Is Well) • Sandi Patty (Bethlehem Morning) • Amy Grant (Breath of Heaven) • Michael Card (Celebrate the Child) • Steven Curtis Chapman (Going Home for Christmas) • Michael English (Mary Did You Know?) • Steve Green (Rose of Bethlehem) • 4Him (A Strange Way to Save the World) • Point of Grace (This Gift) • Scott Wesley Brown (This Little Child) • and more.
00310643 ....$12.95

The Definitive Christmas Collection – 2nd Edition
All the Christmas songs you need in one convenient collection! Over 120 classics in all! Songs include: An Old Fashioned Christmas • Away in a Manger • The Chipmunk Song • Christmas Time Is Here • The Christmas Waltz • Do They Know It's Christmas • Feliz Navidad • The First Noel • Frosty the Snow Man • The Greatest Gift of All • Happy Holiday • A Holly Jolly Christmas • I Saw Mommy Kissing Santa Claus • Jingle-Bell Rock • Mister Santa • My Favorite Things • O Holy Night • Rudolph, The Red-Nosed Reindeer • Santa, Bring My Baby Back (To Me) • Silent Night • Silver Bells • Suzy Snowflake • We Need a Little Christmas • and many more.
00311602 ....$29.95

The Lighter Side of Christmas
42 fun festive favorites, including: Grandma Got Run Over by a Reindeer • A Holly Jolly Christmas • I Guess There Ain't No Santa Claus • I Saw Mommy Kissing Santa Claus • Jingle-Bell Rock • The Merry Christmas Polka • Rockin' Around the Christmas Tree • Rudolph the Red-Nosed Reindeer • That's What I'd Like for Christmas • and more.
00310628 ....$14.95

Ultimate Christmas - 3rd Edition
100 seasonal favorites, including: Auld Lang Syne • Bring a Torch, Jeannette, Isabella • Carol of the Bells • The Chipmunk Song • Christmas Time Is Here • The First Noel • Frosty the Snow Man • Gesù Bambino • Happy Holiday • Happy Xmas (War Is Over) • Hymne • Jesu, Joy of Man's Desiring • Jingle-Bell Rock • March of the Toys • My Favorite Things • The Night Before Christmas Song • Pretty Paper • Silver and Gold • Silver Bells • Suzy Snowflake • What Child Is This • The Wonderful World of Christmas • and more.
00361399 ....$19.95

FOR MORE INFORMATION, SEE YOUR LOCAL MUSIC DEALER,
OR WRITE TO:

HAL•LEONARD®
CORPORATION

7777 W. BLUEMOUND RD. P.O. BOX 13819 MILWAUKEE, WI 53213
http://www.halleonard.com

PRICES, CONTENTS, AND AVAILABILITY SUBJECT TO CHANGE WITHOUT NOTICE.

0703